SUPREME WISDOM

For Developing Nations and Black America
A Parent and Student Course To Economic Stability

R.L.M. Publishing

Prepared By Rasheed L. Muhammad

Acknowledgement

Thanks to Allah (God), who came in the Personage of Master W. Fard Muhammad, the Great Mahdi of the Muslim world and Messiah of the Christians.

I also thank the Honorable Minister Louis Farrakhan Muhammad for his endorsement of the content of the book *"Nation of Islam Decoded: Sciences of Mankind"* from which the material of this course, Supreme Wisdom For Developing Nation and Black America.... derives. Lastly, thanks to the new man, the Honorable Elijah Muhammad, who set the first example by using Supreme Wisdom amongst those who publicly declared themselves to be righteous Muslims in the Western Hemisphere—the Lost and Found members of the Nation of Islam, black man and women of North America.

Table of Content

**Holy is He! He is Allah the One, the Most Supreme
(Quran 39:5)**

Introduction

A mysterious righteous man from Mecca, Arabia gave a six set lesson book to Black America, between 1930 and 1934. These lessons contained many sciences. He said his name was W. D. Fard Muhammad or Mahdi. The name of the lesson book he provided is called "Supreme Wisdom." The first black man to exemplify the necessity of *that* Supreme Wisdom was Elijah Muhammad—Founder of the Nation of Islam in the West. The second black man was Minister Louis Farrakhan Muhammad.

In 1936, the Hon. Elijah Muhammad wrote the following letter to the early founding members of the Nation of Islam regarding the identity of W.D. Fard Muhammad. (See letter on following page)

The Supreme Wisdom Book of the Nation of Islam in the West contains hundreds of fields of study or (ologies) used and applied during our modern times. Her ologies may also be extracted and decoded from both Quran and Bible. The sciences or fields of study herein were calculated to strengthen the mentality of any developing people or nation who will to do so. In fact, some of its fields of study given to the lost and found members of the Nation of Islam, the United States government stole directly from Mr. Elijah Muhammad as late as 1942. Subsequently, European nations including the United States *deploy* such ologies foremost among the many nations on earth today.

Therefore, this course to economic stability is an application designed to compel one to take action to do for self, community and nationhood building. Every session, lesson and discussion pertaining to this course is one of life's higher-sciences. In this manner, any developing people or lost nation will learn how to apply what heretofore has been blocked from their mentality, particularly Black America in general, and Black youth chiefly.

All Praises are due to Allah, who appeared in the Person of

Master W.D. Fard Muhammad Born February 26, 1877

"WILDERNESS OF NORTH AMERICA"

February 26, 1936

Written and sent to #1 Michigan by the Honorable Elijah Muhammad,

Servant of Allah

This day February 26, 1877, Fifty nine years ago, in Heaven the Holy City Mecca, a Savior was born.

From the bearers of Heaven's throne, a voice raised high and mighty Master W.D. Fard Muhammad, have been born the mighty King.

Born...to save me, and my people who were lost, Blind, Deaf, and Dumb. Dead to the knowledged of everything.

Born..Hath he, to intercede, for me, and my people in this Judgement Day.

Born...to give life to me and my people, that we might live.

Born...to give Freedom to me, and my people, who were slaves to devils in this wicked Hell of North America.

Born...to give Justice, to we lost founds, who never knew what it was before.

Born...to give Equality with the Angels of Paradise.

Born...to save the fallen sons of the Tribe of Shabazz from the wicked grasp of Yakub's made devil and satan.

Born...to destroy with unquenchless fire, the enemy of we Lost People that the work of Yakub's made devil will never revive.

Born...to unite the Lost Sheep who went astray in 1555 with the 4,400,000,000 of his Nation.

Born...to restore all Black Mankind into one Love together.

Born...The Lord of the Worlds!

Born...to destroy the old world; and bring in the new world.

Born...the Wisest of all, the most Merciful, the most Loving, the Almighty, the knower of what is in man's heart, the Doer of what he pleases...There is no God but Him, in the Earth, not in the heavens above the Earth. I shall forever remember this day, the 26th of February, 1877, and my off spring too. To keep a fast of joy with all my poor lost found Nation, whom this, Our Savior the King was born; I shall not eat any food this day until the sun goes down. This I will do, that my heart, and my body be not hindered, from giving praise to my King that was born this day, whose light of Love, Freedom, Justice, and Equality, is greater to me than the Sun, Moon, and Stars.

Now come all you lost founds, and praise the name of our Savior and King, who was born, and we have reclaimed our own.

He gave to us his Holy Name and calls everyone of us by our own. All praise be to Our Savior, the Almighty ALLAH. The Strong, the Giver of Life. Praise him, you who have reclaimed your own, and know him as your Savior and King. Forever and ever, let the Universe Praise Him.

[source:] http://muhammadspeaks.com/HappySavDay1936.html

This course, "SUPREME WISDOM For Developing Nations and Black America: *A Parent and Student Course To Economic Stability*" is fit for parents and students. It is also recommended to read *"Nation of Islam Decoded: Sciences of Mankind"* by Rasheed L. Muhammad to expand upon the nature, function and purpose for this course, which further demonstrates the value of Elijah Muhammad and his trustee, Minister Louis Farrakhan's assignment among America's former slave descendants—*African Americans*.

In addition, this course provides the reader with some essential fundamentals to prepare and to qualify for nation building—**high level nation building skills**. Higher fields of science are now being applied by all *modern nations* on earth including former third world nations, such as China, Japan, India, various African nations as well as other dark skin nations around the globe. Their progress is being gained through younger generations during these modern times.

Directions to complete this course:

Step 1: Parents and *Students* must begin course/work booklet from the Actual Fact lesson plan to find a field of study that he or she desires to achieve for self, community and economic stability. *Step 2:* After finding a field of study you must:

(1) name the area of study in the field of its "ology"

(2) write how it compares to the Supreme Wisdom Lesson Book

(3) name what industries, services and businesses may derive from the field of study

(4) name a corporate, personal or national economic and social potential that the field of study may yields

(5) name what educational courses are essential to complete in order to make a nation and/or person achieve economic and self realization from the skill

For example, one of the Nation of Islam's Supreme Wisdom Lessons reads: ***"The producing land is 29,000,000 square miles".*** The question is: is the usefulness of ***Producing Land*** just a philosophical quotation or a debatable point? If you cannot describe a value to the question, this course will demonstrate the true value of ***useful land***. The following outline demonstrates the science or ologies behind the nature, function and purpose of ***useful land***. For instance:

Field of Study: *Agronomics*

(a) **Area of Study**: *Study of productivity of land*

(b) ***Supreme Wisdom Actual Fact Book* #14 states**: *The producing land is 29,000,000 square miles.*

(c) **Derived Industries**: *Soybeans* (***Internet search engine: soybean industry for more details***)

(d) **Economic (or social benefit) potential**: *2005 72.1 million acres planted, $16 Billion Farm cash receipts and production, 435 million bushels exported to China. People can eat and work.*

(e) **Educational requirements**: *Mathematics, Physical Life Science, Agricultural Science, Economics, Biology, Principles of Crop Production..... plus...*

Is Agronomics a worthwhile field to study or "ology"? Is it an attainable goal that can be and must be fulfilled or carried into reality by a well-trained, educated network of systems and people? Can any developing nation benefit from useful land (Agronomics) by doing for self, community and strengthening its economic stability?

As you may see, the ***usefulness of Producing Land*** is not just a philosophical quotation or a debatable mathematical point. It takes Brainpower to reclaim land to serve our human needs, for that matter it takes employing higher sciences.

SUPREME WISDOM For Developing Nations and Black America: *A Parent and Student Course To Economic Stability* will require research and answers from you. This course only contains some of the N.O.I. secret lessons. Your answers should not be long, drawn out or philosophical. So please begin "Right Now"! (Smile)

Assignment 1

Actual Facts

Instructions: Choose at least 4 areas to research and complete answers on the lines provided.

Lessons of W.D. Fard | Corresponding Sciences/Fields of Study

[4] The area of the Land is 57,255,000 miles.

[14] The producing land is 29,000,000 square miles.

[13] The deserts are 4,861,000 square miles.

[10] The hills and mountains cover 14,000,000 square mile.

gromatics	science of surveying
geomorphogeny	study of the origins of land forms
agronomics	study of productivity of land
agrology	study of agricultural soils
agrostology	science or study of grasses
geoponics	study of agriculture
edaphology	study of soils
eremology	study of deserts
phytology	study of plants; botany
orology	study of mountains
eremology	study of deserts
mineralogy	study of minerals

"We sent down from the sky blessed water whereby We caused to grow gardens, grains for harvest, tall palm-trees with their spathes, piled one above the other --- sustenance for (Our) servants. Therewith We gave (new) life to a dead land. So will be the emergence from the tombs." Holy Quran 23:18-19

1. Field of Study: _____

a) Area of Study:

_____

_____

_____

_____

b) Actual Fact #____:

c) Derived Industries:

_____

_____

_____

_____

d) Economic (or social benefit) potential:

_____

_____

_____

_____

e) Educational requirements:

_____

_____

_____

_____

2. Field of Study: _____

a) Area of Study:

_____

_____

_____

_____

b) Actual Fact #____:

c) Derived Industries:

_____

_____

_____

_____

d) Economic (or social benefit) potential:

_____

_____

_____

_____

e) Educational requirements:

_____

_____

_____

_____

3. Field of Study: _____

a) Area of Study:

b) Actual Fact #____:

c) Derived Industries:

d) Economic (or social benefit) potential:

e) Educational requirements:

4. Field of Study: _____

a) Area of Study:

_____

_____

b) Actual Fact #____:

c) Derived Industries:

_____

_____

_____

_____

d) Economic (or social benefit) potential:

_____

_____

_____

_____

e) Educational requirements:

_____

_____

_____

_____

[7] The Atlantic Ocean covers 41,321,000 square miles.

[6] The Pacific Ocean cover 68,634,000 square miles.

[9] Lakes and rivers cover 1,000,000 square miles.

[5] The area of the water is 139,685,000 square miles.

oceanology	study of oceans
selenology	study of the moon
phycology	study of algae and seaweeds
fluviology	study of watercourses
piscatology	study of fishes
potamology	study of rivers
hydrography	study of investigating bodies of water
ichthyology	study of fish
limnobiology	study of freshwater ecosystems
limnology	study of bodies of fresh water
microanatomy	study of microscopic tissues
microbiology	study of microscopic organisms
hydrobiology	study of aquatic organisms

"He is the one who has let free the two bodies of flowing water, one sweet and palatable, and the other salty and bitter. And He has made between them a barrier and a forbidding partition". (Holy Quran 25:53)

1. Field of Study: _____

a) Area of Study:

_____

_____

_____

_____

b) Actual Fact #____:

c) Derived Industries:

_____

_____

_____

_____

d) Economic (or social benefit) potential:

_____

_____

_____

_____

e) Educational requirements:

_____

_____

_____

_____

2. Field of Study: _____

a) Area of Study:

_____

_____

_____

_____

b) Actual Fact #____:

c) Derived Industries:

_____

_____

_____

_____

d) Economic (or social benefit) potential:

_____

_____

_____

e) Educational requirements:

_____

_____

_____

_____

3. *Field of Study*: _____

a) Area of Study:

_____

_____

_____

_____

b) Actual Fact #____:

c) Derived Industries:

_____

_____

_____

_____

d) Economic (or social benefit) potential:

_____

_____

_____

_____

e) Educational requirements:

_____

_____

_____

_____

[18] *Light travels at the rate of 186,000 miles per second.*

[19] *Sound travels at the rate of 1,120 feet per second.*

optics	study of light
dioptrics	study of light refraction
acoustics	science of sound
catacoustics	science of echoes or reflected sounds

"Allah is the Light (noor) of the heavens and the earth. The Parable of His Light (noor) is as if there were a Niche and within it a Lamp (misbah): the Lamp (misbah) enclosed in Glass: the glass as it were a brilliant star: Lit from a blessed Tree, an Olive, neither of the east nor of the west, whose oil is well-nigh uminous, though fire scarce touched it: Light (noor) upon Light (noor)! God does guide whom He will to His Light (noor): God does set forth Parables for men: and God does know all things." (Holy Quran 24:35)

1. *Field of Study*: _____

    a) Area of Study:

_____

_____

_____

    b) Actual Fact #____:

c) Derived Industries:

_____

_____

_____

_____

d) Economic (or social benefit) potential:

_____

_____

_____

_____

e) Educational requirements:

_____

_____

_____

_____

2. *Field of Study*: _____

a) Area of Study:

_____

_____

_____

_____

b) Actual Fact #____:

c) Derived Industries:

_____

_____

_____

_____

d) Economic (or social benefit) potential:

_____

_____

_____

_____

e) Educational requirements:

_____

_____

_____

_____

3. *Field of Study*: _____

a) Area of Study:

_____

_____

_____

_____

b) Actual Fact #____:

c) Derived Industries:

_____

_____

_____

_____

d) Economic (or social benefit) potential:

_____

_____

_____

_____

e) Educational requirements:

_____

_____

_____

_____

[16] The Earth is 93,000,000 from the Sun.

[20] The Diameter of the Sun is 853,000 miles.

heliology	science of the sun
horology	science of time measurement
horography	art of constructing sundials or clocks
calorifics	study of heat

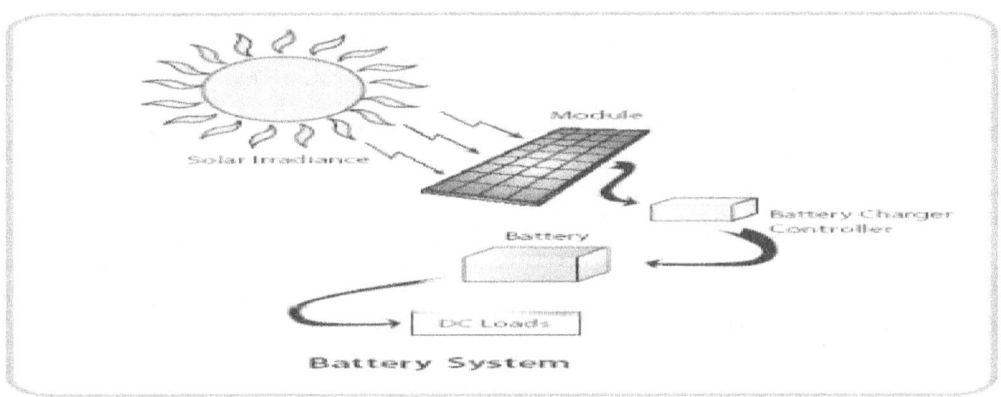

"By the sun and its brightness. The moon that follows it. The day that reveals. The night that covers. The sky and Him who built it. The earth and Him who sustains it. The soul and Him who created it. Then showed it what is evil and what is good." (Holy Quran 91:1-8)

1. Field of Study: _____

a) Area of Study:

_____

_____

_____

_____

b) Actual Fact #____:

c) Derived Industries:

_____

_____

_____

_____

d) Economic (or social benefit) potential:

_____

_____

_____

_____

e) Educational requirements:

_____

_____

_____

_____

2. *Field of Study*: _____

a) Area of Study:

_____

_____

_____

_____

b) Actual Fact #____:

c) Derived Industries:

_____

_____

_____

_____

d) Economic (or social benefit) potential:

_____

_____

_____

_____

e) Educational requirements:

_____

_____

_____

_____

3. Field of Study: _____

a) Area of Study:

_____

_____

_____

_____

b) Actual Fact #____:

c) Derived Industries:

_____

_____

_____

_____

d) Economic (or social benefit) potential:

_____

_____

_____

_____

e) Educational requirements:

_____

_____

_____

_____

4. *Field of Study*: _____

a) Area of Study:

_____

_____

_____

_____

b) Actual Fact #____:

c) Derived Industries:

_____

_____

_____

_____

d) Economic (or social benefit) potential:

_____

_____

_____

_____

e) Educational requirements:

_____

_____

_____

_____

Assignment 2

Student Enrollment (Rules of Islam)

Instructions: Choose at least 2 areas to research and then complete answers on the lines provided.

Lessons of W.D. Fard   Corresponding Sciences/Fields of Study

1. Who is the Original Man?
Answer: The Original Man is the Asiatic Black Man, the Maker, the Owner, the Cream of the Planet Earth, God of the Universe.

2. Who is the Colored Man?
Answer: The Colored Man is the Caucasian (White man) or Yacob's grafted devil, the Skunk of the Planet Earth.

ethnogeny	study of origins of races or ethnic groups
anthropology	study of human cultures
ekistics	study of human settlement
palaeoanthropology	study of early humans
archology	science of the origins of government

"Or dost thou reflect that the Companions of the Cave...We relate to thee their story in truth: they were youths who believed in their Lord, and We advanced them in guidance:" (Holy Quran 18:9;13)

1. Field of Study: _____

a) Area of Study:

_____

_____

_____

_____

b) Student Enrollment #_____:

c) Derived Industries:

_____

_____

_____

_____

d) Economic (or social benefit) potential:

_____

_____

_____

_____

e) Educational requirements:

_____

_____

_____

_____

2. Field of Study: _____

a) Area of Study:

_____

_____

_____

_____

b) Student Enrollment #____:

c) Derived Industries:

_____

_____

_____

_____

d) Economic (or social benefit) potential:

_____

_____

_____

_____

e) Educational requirements:

_____

_____

_____

_____

3. Field of Study: _____

a) Area of Study:

_____

_____

_____

_____

b) Student Enrollment #____:

c) Derived Industries:

_____

_____

_____

_____

d) Economic (or social benefit) potential:

_____

_____

_____

_____

e) Educational requirements:

_____

_____

_____

_____

4. Field of Study: _____

a) Area of Study:

_____

_____

_____

_____

b) Student Enrollment #____:

c) Derived Industries:

_____

_____

_____

_____

d) Economic (or social benefit) potential:

_____

_____

_____

_____

e) Educational requirements:

_____

_____

_____

_____

3. What is the population of the Original Nation in the Wilderness of North America and all over the Planet Earth?
Answer: The Population of the Original Nation in the wilderness of North America is 17,000,000 with the 2,000,000 Indians make it, 19,000,000. All over the Planet Earth is 4,400,000,000.

larithmics	study of population statistics
sociology	study of society
geotechnics	study of increasing habitability of the earth

4. What is the population of the Colored People in the wilderness of North America and all over the Planet Earth?
Answer: The Population of the Colored People in the wilderness of North America is 103,000,000 million. All over the Planet Earth is 400,000,000.

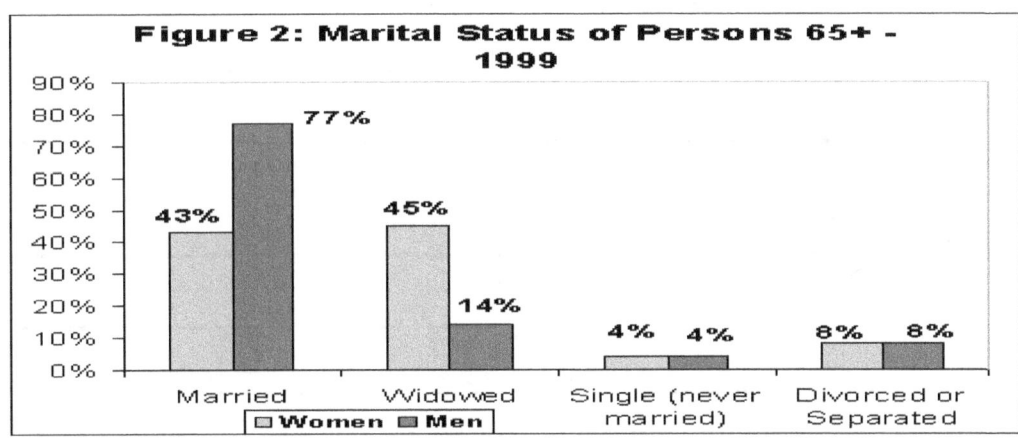

Figure 2: Marital Status of Persons 65+ – 1999

"O humankind! We have created you from a male and a female, and made you into nations and tribes, that you may know one another. Verily, the most honorable of you with Allah is that who has At-Taqwa. Verily, Allah is All-knowing, All-Aware." (Holy Quran 49:13)

1. Field of Study: _____

    a) Area of Study:

_____

_____

_____

_____

b) Student Enrollment #____:

c) Derived Industries:

_____

_____

_____

_____

d) Economic (or social benefit) potential:

_____

_____

_____

_____

e) Educational requirements:

_____

_____

_____

_____

2. *Field of Study*: _____

a) Area of Study:

_____

_____

_____

_____

b) Student Enrollment #____:

c) Derived Industries:

_____

_____

_____

_____

d) Economic (or social benefit) potential:

_____

_____

_____

_____

e) Educational requirements:

_____

_____

_____

_____

6. How much of the useful land is used by the Original Man?
Answer: The Original Man uses 23,000,000 square miles.

7. How much of the useful land is used by the Colored Man?
Answer: The Colored Man uses 6,000,000 square miles.

agronomics	study of productivity of land
microclimatology	study of local climates

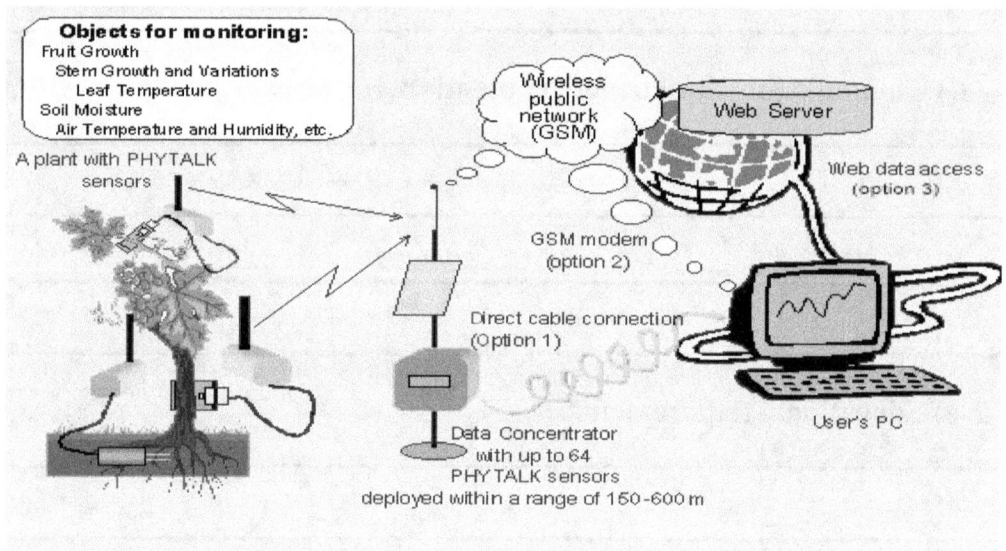

"Seek not mischief in the land, for Allah loves not those who do mischief."
(Quran 28:77)

1. *Field of Study*: _____

a) Area of Study:

_____

_____

_____

_____

b) Student Enrollment #____:

c) Derived Industries:

_____

_____

_____

_____

d) Economic (or social benefit) potential:

_____

_____

_____

_____

e) Educational requirements:

_____

_____

_____

_____

2. Field of Study: _____

a) Area of Study:

_____

_____

_____

_____

b) Student Enrollment #____:

c) Derived Industries:

_____

_____

_____

_____

d) Economic (or social benefit) potential:

_____

_____

_____

_____

e) Educational requirements:

_____

_____

_____

_____

9. What is the birth record of the said, Nation of Islam?
Answer: The said, Nation of Islam has no birth record. It has no beginning nor ending

10. What is the birth record of said, others than Islam?
Answer: Buddhism is 35,000 years old. Christianity is 551 years old.

soteriology	study of theological salvation
theology	study of religion; religious doctrine
patrology	study of early Christianity

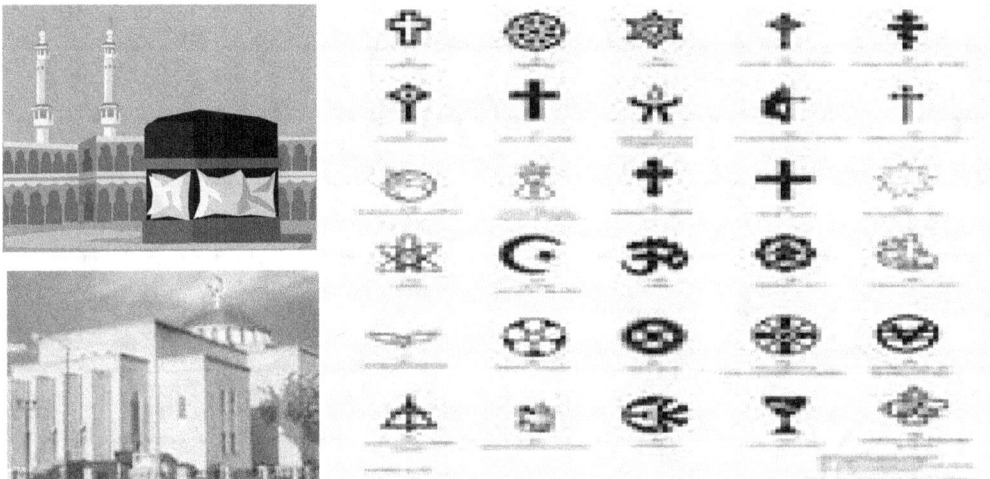

"If Allah so willed, he would have made you a single People, but his plan is to test each of you separately, in what He has given to each of you: so strive in all virtues as in you are in a race. The goal of all of you is to Allah. It is He that will show you the truth of the matters in which ye dispute." (Qur'an 5:48)

1. Field of Study: _____

   a) Area of Study:

_____

_____

_____

_____

   b) Student Enrollment #____:

c) Derived Industries:

_____

_____

_____

_____

d) Economic (or social benefit) potential:

_____

_____

_____

_____

e) Educational requirements:

_____

_____

_____

_____

2. Field of Study: _____

a) Area of Study:

_____

_____

_____

_____

b) Student Enrollment #____:

c) Derived Industries:

_____

_____

_____

_____

d) Economic (or social benefit) potential:

_____

_____

_____

_____

e) Educational requirements:

_____

_____

_____

_____

Assignment 3

Lost Found Muslim Lesson NO. 1

Instructions: Choose at least 3 areas to research and then complete answers on the lines provided.

Lessons of W.D. Fard: Answered by Elijah Muhammad   Corresponding Sciences/Fields of Study

1. Why isn't the devil settled on the best part of the planet Earth?
ANS:- Because the earth belongs to the original black man. And knowing that the devil was wicked and there would not be any peace among them, he put him out in the worst part of the earth and kept the best part preserved for himself ever since he made it. The best part is in Arabia at the Holy City Mecca. The colored man or Caucasian is the devil....

hamartiology	study of sin
irenology	the study of peace
sociology	study of society
sociobiology	study of biological basis of human behaviour
characterology	study of development of character

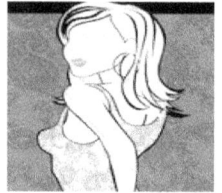   

"O Children of Adam! Let not Satan seduce you as he caused your (first) parents to ..." (Holy Quran 7:27)

1. Field of Study: _____

   a) Area of Study:

_____

_____

_____

_____

b) Lost Found Muslim Lesson NO. 1, *No.* ____:

c) Derived Industries:

_____

_____

_____

_____

d) Economic (or social benefit) potential:

_____

_____

_____

_____

e) Educational requirements:

_____

_____

_____

_____

2. *Field of Study*: _____

a) Area of Study:

_____

_____

_____

_____

b) Lost Found Muslim Lesson NO. 1, *No.* ____:

c) Derived Industries:

_____

_____

_____

_____

d) Economic (or social benefit) potential:

_____

_____

_____

_____

e) Educational requirements:

_____

_____

_____

_____

3. Field of Study: _____

a) Area of Study:

_____

_____

_____

_____

b) Lost Found Muslim Lesson NO. 1, *No.* ____:

c) Derived Industries:

_____

_____

_____

_____

d) Economic (or social benefit) potential:

_____

_____

_____

_____

e) Educational requirements:

_____

_____

_____

_____

4. Why did we run Yacob and his made devil from the root of civilization, over the hot desert, into the cave of West Asia, as they now call it, Europe? What is the meaning of Eu and Rope? How long ago? What did the devil bring with him? What kind of life did he live? And how long before Mossa came to teach the devil of the forgotten Tricknollegy?

ctetology	study of the inheritance of acquired characteristics
psychognosy	study of mentality, personality or character
polemology	study of war
etymology	study of origins of words
demology	study of human behaviour

"They question thee (O Muhammad) with regard to warfare in the sacred month. Say: Warfare therein is a great (transgression), but to turn (men) from the way of Allah, and to disbelieve in Him and in the Inviolable Place of Worship, and to expel His people thence, is a greater with Allah; for persecution is worse than killing. And they will not cease from fighting against you till they have made you renegades from your religion, if they can. And whoso becometh a renegade and dieth in his disbelief: such are they whose works have fallen both in the world and the Hereafter. Such are rightful owners of the Fire: they will abide therein." (Holy Quran 2:217)

1. Field of Study: _____

a) Area of Study:

_____

_____

_____

_____

b) Lost Found Muslim Lesson NO. 1, *No.* ____:

c) Derived Industries:

_____

_____

_____

_____

d) Economic (or social benefit) potential:

_____

_____

_____

_____

e) Educational requirements:

_____

_____

_____

_____

2. Field of Study: _____

a) Area of Study:

_____

_____

_____

_____

b) Lost Found Muslim Lesson NO. 1, *No.* ____:

c) Derived Industries:

_____

_____

_____

_____

d) Economic (or social benefit) potential:

_____

_____

_____

e) Educational requirements:

_____

_____

_____

_____

3. Field of Study: _____

a) Area of Study:

_____

_____

_____

_____

b) Lost Found Muslim Lesson NO. 1, *No.* ____:

c) Derived Industries:

_____

_____

_____

_____

d) Economic (or social benefit) potential:

_____

_____

_____

e) Educational requirements:

_____

_____

_____

_____

14. What is the meaning of M.G.T. and G.C.C? **ANS.**-Muslim Girls' Training and General Civilization Class. This was the name given to the training of women and girls in North America; how to keep house, how to rear children, how to take care of their husbands, sew, cook, and, in general, how to act at home and abroad. ...

aretaics	the science of virtue
characterology	study of development of character
hygiastics	science of health and hygiene
magirics	art of cookery
neonatology	study of newborn babies
oikology	science of housekeeping
paedology	study of children
paedotrophy	art of rearing children
sexology	study of sexual behaviour
proxemics	study of man's need for personal space

"Alif Laam Raa. A book which we have revealed to you (Muhammad) so that you may lead the people from out of the darknesses into the light by their Lord's leave to the path of the All-Mighty, the Praiseworthy." (Holy Quran 14:1)

1. Field of Study: _____

a) Area of Study:

_____

_____

_____

_____

b) Lost Found Muslim Lesson NO. 1, *No.* ____:

c) Derived Industries:

_____

_____

_____

_____

d) Economic (or social benefit) potential:

_____

_____

_____

_____

e) Educational requirements:

_____

_____

_____

_____

2. *Field of Study*: _____

a) Area of Study:

_____

_____

_____

_____

b) Lost Found Muslim Lesson NO. 1, *No.* ____:

c) Derived Industries:

_____

_____

_____

_____

d) Economic (or social benefit) potential:

_____

_____

_____

_____

e) Educational requirements:

_____

_____

_____

_____

3. *Field of Study*: _____

a) Area of Study:

_____

_____

_____

_____

b) Lost Found Muslim Lesson NO. 1, *No.* ____:

c) Derived Industries:

_____

_____

_____

_____

d) Economic (or social benefit) potential:

_____

_____

_____

e) Educational requirements:

_____

_____

_____

_____

4. Field of Study: _____

a) Area of Study:

_____

_____

_____

_____

b) Lost Found Muslim Lesson NO. 1, *No.* ____:

c) Derived Industries:

_____

_____

_____

_____

d) Economic (or social benefit) potential:

_____

_____

_____

_____

e) Educational requirements:

_____

_____

_____

_____

Assignment 4

Lost Found Muslim Lesson NO. 2

Instructions: Choose at least 2 areas to research and then complete answers on the lines provided.

Lessons of W.D. Fard: Answered by Elijah Muhammad   Corresponding Sciences/Fields of Study

1. Who made the Holy Koran or Bible? How long ago? Will you tell us why does Islam renew her history every twenty-five thousand years?

codicology	study of manuscripts
pisteology	science or study of faith
soteriology	study of theological salvation
historiography	study of writing history
cryptology	study of codes

"Indeed, the transgressors have followed their own opinions, without knowledge. Who then can guide those who have been sent astray by GOD? No one can ever help them. Therefore, you shall devote yourself to the religion of strict monotheism. Such is the natural instinct placed into the people by GOD. Such creation of GOD will never change. This is the perfect religion, but most people do not know. You shall submit to Him, reverence Him, observe the Contact Prayers (Salat), and - whatever you do - do not ever fall into idol worship. (Do not fall in idol worship,) like those who divide their religion into sects; each party rejoicing with what they have." (Holy Quran 30:29-32)

1. Field of Study: _____

   a) Area of Study:

_____

_____

_____

_____

b) Lost Found Muslim Lesson NO. 2, *No.* ____:

c) Derived Industries:

_____

_____

_____

_____

d) Economic (or social benefit) potential:

_____

_____

_____

_____

e) Educational requirements:

_____

_____

_____

_____

2. *Field of Study*: _____

a) Area of Study:

_____

_____

_____

_____

b) Lost Found Muslim Lesson NO. 2, *No.* ____:

c) Derived Industries:

_____

_____

_____

_____

d) Economic (or social benefit) potential:

_____

_____

_____

_____

e) Educational requirements:

_____

_____

_____

_____

3. *Field of Study*: _____

a) Area of Study:

_____

_____

_____

_____

b) Lost Found Muslim Lesson NO. 2, *No.* ____:

c) Derived Industries:

_____

_____

_____

_____

d) Economic (or social benefit) potential:

_____

_____

_____

_____

e) Educational requirements:

_____

_____

_____

_____

3. What makes rain, hail, snow and earthquakes?

climatology	study of climate
hydrometeorology	study of atmospheric moisture
hyetology	science of rainfall
hygrology	study of humidity
meteorology	study of weather
nephology	study of clouds
astrometeorology	study of effect of stars on climate
seismology	study of earthquakes
stratigraphy	study of geological layers or strata

"Do not you see that God drives the clouds, then joins them together, then piles them on each other, then you see the rain comes forth from between them. And He sends down hail from the sky, where there are mountains of it. And strikes those with it whom He will and diverts it from whomever He wills. The vivid flash of its lightning nearly blinds the sight." (Holy Quran 24:43)

1. Field of Study: _____

a) Area of Study:

_____

_____

_____

_____

b) Lost Found Muslim Lesson NO. 2, *No.* ____:

c) Derived Industries:

_____

_____

_____

_____

d) Economic (or social benefit) potential:

_____

_____

_____

_____

e) Educational requirements:

_____

_____

_____

_____

2. *Field of Study*: _____

a) Area of Study:

_____

_____

_____

_____

b) Actual Fact #____:

c) Derived Industries:

_____

_____

_____

_____

d) Economic (or social benefit) potential:

_____

_____

_____

_____

e) Educational requirements:

_____

_____

_____

_____

3. Field of Study: _____

a) Area of Study:

_____

_____

_____

_____

b) Lost Found Muslim Lesson NO. 2, *No.* ____:

c) Derived Industries:

_____

_____

_____

_____

d) Economic (or social benefit) potential:

_____

_____

_____

_____

e) Educational requirements:

_____

_____

_____

_____

4. Field of Study: _____

a) Area of Study:

_____

_____

_____

_____

b) Lost Found Muslim Lesson NO. 2, *No.* ____:

c) Derived Industries:

_____

_____

_____

_____

d) Economic (or social benefit) potential:

_____

_____

_____

_____

e) Educational requirements:

_____

_____

_____

_____

Lessons of W.D. Fard: Answered by Elijah Muhammad   Corresponding Sciences/Fields of Study

9. Why does the devil teach the eighty-five percent that a mystery God brings all this? **ANS** – To conceal the true God, which is the Son of man, and make slaves out of the 85% by keeping them worshipping something he knows they cannot see (invisible), and he lives and makes himself rich from their labor. The 85% know that it rains, hails and snows; also, hear it thunder above his head, but they do not try to learn who is it that causes all of this to happen by letting the 5% teach them. He believes in the 10% on face value.

brontology	scientific study of thunder
electrostatics	study of static electricity

"He is the One who shows you the lightning as a source of fear, as well as hope, and He initiates the loaded clouds. The thunder praises His glory, and so do the angels, out of reverence for Him. He sends the lightning bolts, which strike in accordance with His will. Yet, they argue about GOD, though His power is awesome." (Holy Quran 13:12-13)

1. Field of Study: _____

   a) Area of Study:

_____

_____

_____

_____

   b) Lost Found Muslim Lesson NO. 2, *No.* ____:

   c) Derived Industries:

_____

_____

_____

_____

   d) Economic (or social benefit) potential:

_____

_____

_____

_____

   e) Educational requirements:

_____

_____

14. Who is the 85%?
ANS – The uncivilized people; poison animal eaters; slaves from mental death and power; people who do not know the living God or their origin in this world, and they worship that they know not what – who are easily led in the wrong direction, but hard to lead into the right direction.

| archelogy | the study of first principles |
| genealogy | study of descent of families |

"And (O Muhammad) recite to them (the Jews) the story of the two sons of Adam (Abel and Cain) in truth; when each offered a sacrifice to God, it was accepted from the one but not from the other. The latter said to the former; 'I will surely kill you. "So the self (base desires) of the other (latter one) encouraged him and made fair seeming to him the murder of his brother; he murdered him and became one of the losers." (Holy Quran 5:27-28)

1. Field of Study: _____

   a) Area of Study:

_____

_____

_____

   b) Lost Found Muslim Lesson NO. 2, *No.* ____:

   c) Derived Industries:

_____

_____

d) Economic (or social benefit) potential:

_____

_____

_____

_____

e) Educational requirements:

_____

_____

_____

_____

Lessons of W.D. Fard: Answered by Elijah Muhammad	Corresponding Sciences/Fields of Study

15. Who is the 10%?
ANS – The rich; the slave-makers of the poor, who teach the poor lies – to believe that the almighty, true and living God is a spook and cannot be seen by the physical eye. Otherwise known as the blood-sucker of the poor...

pseudology	art or science of lying

"Nor irreverently mix up the truth guiding into all truth and poison it with what you forge of falsehood, nor conceal the truth when you know it conforms with fact and agrees with reality". (Quran 2:42)

1. Field of Study: _____

a) Area of Study:

_____

_____

b) Lost Found Muslim Lesson NO. 2, *No.* ____:

c) Derived Industries:

d) Economic (or social benefit) potential:

e) Educational requirements:

30. Tell us what and how the devil is made?
ANS – The devil is made from the original people by grafting (separating the germs)...
In the black man, there exists two germs: one a Black germ, and one – a brown germ.
Yacob, with his law on birth control, separated the brown germs from the black man and grafted it into a white by destroying the black germ. After following this process for six hundred years, the germ became white, and weak and was no more original. And by thinning the original blood, it became weak, and wicked, and it is no more the same. Thus, this is the way Yacob made the devil.

spermology	study of seeds
hematology	study of blood

"We created man from an extract of clay, then we made him as a drop in a place of settlement, firmly fixed. Then we made the drop into an alaqah (leech, suspended thing and blood clot), then we made the alaqah into a mudgah (chewed-like substance)..." (Quran, 23:12-14)

1. Field of Study: _____

    a) Area of Study:

_____

_____

_____

_____

    b) Lost Found Muslim Lesson NO. 2, *No.* ____:

    c) Derived Industries:

_____

_____

_____

_____

d) Economic (or social benefit) potential:

_____

_____

_____

_____

e) Educational requirements:

_____

_____

_____

_____

| Lessons of W.D. Fard: Answered by Elijah Muhammad | Corresponding Sciences/Fields of Study |

38. Then why did God make devil?
ANS – To show for his power, that he is all wise and righteous. That he could make a devil, which is weak and wicked, and give the devil power to rule the Earth for six thousand years and, then destroy the devil in one day without falling a victim to the devil's civilization. Otherwise to show and prove that Allah is the God, always has been and always will be.

| deontology | the theory or study of moral obligation |

"There was a group of Satanic conspirators, the hypocrites, who praised the disbelievers' actions, "You cannot be overcome by any people today, and we will be fighting along with you as allies." But as soon as the two armies came face to face, they turned back on their heels and fled, saying, "We disown you, We see what you don't. We are afraid of Allah Who has instilled faith in the hearts of the believers. Allah is strict in punishment." (Holy Quran 8:48)

1. Field of Study: _____

a) Area of Study:

_____

_____

_____

_____

b) Lost Found Muslim Lesson NO. 2, *No.* ____:

c) Derived Industries:

_____

_____

_____

_____

d) Economic (or social benefit) potential:

_____

_____

_____

_____

e) Educational requirements:

_____

_____

_____

_____

Assignment 5

Problems

Instructions: Choose from 2 to 4 areas to research and then complete answers on the lines provided.

1. The uncle of Mr. W.D. Fard lived in the wilderness of North America and he lived other than his own self, therefore, his pulse beat seventy-eight times per minute and this killed him in forty-five years of age. How many times did his pulse beat in forty-five years?

sphygmology	study of the pulse
symptomatology	study of symptoms of illness

"The pains of labour drove her to the trunk of a date-palm. She [Maryam] said, "Oh if only I had died before this time and was something discarded and forgotten!" A voice called out to her from under her, "Do not grieve! Your Lord has placed a small stream at your feet. Shake the trunk of the palm towards you and fresh, ripe dates will drop down onto you. Eat and drink and delight your eyes..." (Qur'an, 19:23-26)

1. Field of Study: _____

   a) Area of Study:

_____

_____

_____

_____

   b) Problem No. ____ :

   c) Derived Industries:

_____

_____

_____

_____

d) Economic (or social benefit) potential:

_____

_____

_____

_____

e) Educational requirements:

_____

_____

_____

_____

2. *Field of Study*: _____

a) Area of Study:

_____

_____

_____

_____

b) Problem No.____:

c) Derived Industries:

_____

_____

_____

_____

d) Economic (or social benefit) potential:

_____

_____

_____

_____

e) Educational requirements:

_____

_____

_____

_____

2. The wife of Mr. W.D. Fard's uncle, in the wilderness of North America, weighs other than herself, therefore, she has rheumatism, headaches, pain in all joints, and cannot walk up to the store. She is troubled frequently with high Blood pressure and registers more thirty-two. Her pulse is nearly eighty times per minute and she died at the age of forty-seven. How many times did her pulse beat in forty-seven years?

arthrology	study of joints
aceology	therapeutics
angiology	study of blood flow and lymphatic system
cardiology	study of the heart
desmology	study of ligaments

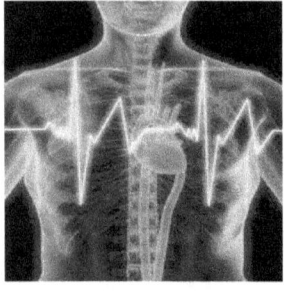
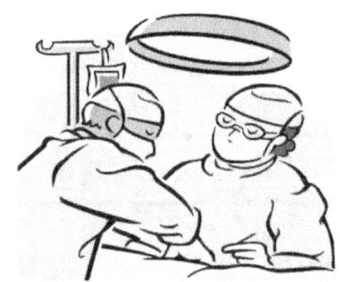

"God has sent down the best discourse as a Book, fully consistent within itself, oft-repeated, whereat shiver the skins of those who fear their Lord; then their skins and hearts soften to the remembrance of God." (Quran 39:23)

1. Field of Study: _____

a) Area of Study:

_____

_____

_____

_____

b) Problem No. ____:

c) Derived Industries:

_____

_____

d) Economic (or social benefit) potential:

_____

_____

_____

_____

e) Educational requirements:

_____

_____

_____

_____

2. Field of Study: _____

a) Area of Study:

_____

_____

_____

_____

b) Problem No. ____:

c) Derived Industries:

_____

_____

_____

_____

d) Economic (or social benefit) potential:

_____

_____

_____

_____

e) Educational requirements:

_____

_____

_____

_____

3. *Field of Study*: _____

a) Area of Study:

_____

_____

_____

_____

b) Problem No.____:

c) Derived Industries:

_____

_____

d) Economic (or social benefit) potential:

_____

_____

_____

_____

e) Educational requirements:

_____

_____

_____

_____

Lessons of W.D. Fard   Corresponding Sciences/Fields of Study

3. A Sheep contains fourteen square feet. One-tenth of a square inch contains fourteen thousand hairs. How many will the fourteen square feet contain?

zoonomy	animal physiology
stoichiology	science of elements of animal tissues
trichology	study of hair and its disorders

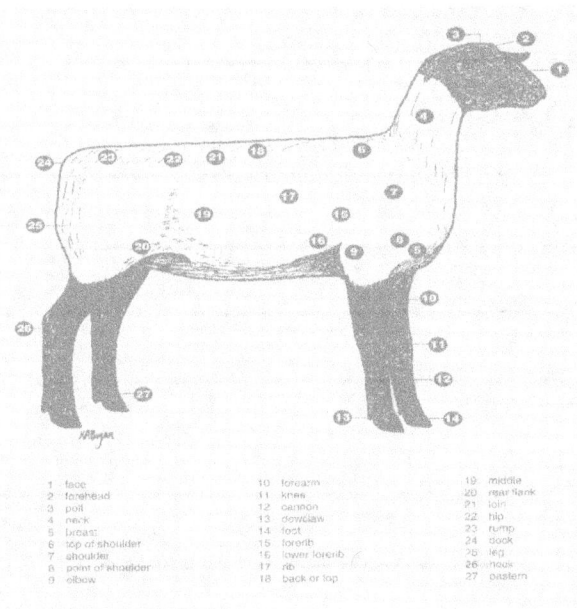

1	face	10	forearm	19	middle
2	forehead	11	knee	20	rear flank
3	poll	12	cannon	21	loin
4	neck	13	dewclaw	22	hip
5	breast	14	foot	23	rump
6	top of shoulder	15	forerib	24	dock
7	shoulder	16	lower forerib	25	leg
8	point of shoulder	17	rib	26	hock
9	elbow	18	back or top	27	pastern

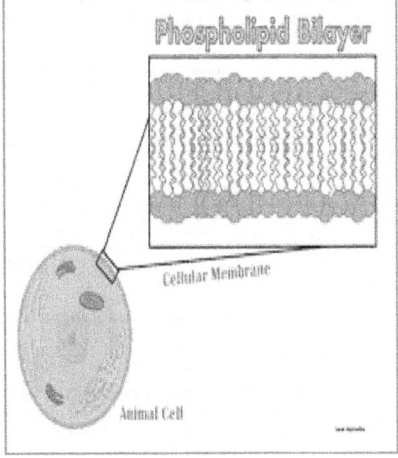

Phospholipid Bilayer

Cellular Membrane

Animal Cell

"(God) created cattle for you and (you find) in them warmth, useful services and food, sense o! beauty when you bring them home and when you take them to pasture. They bear your heavy loads to lands you could not reach except with great personal effort, Verily, your Lord is compassionate and Merciful; (He created) horses, mules and donkeys for you to ride and for ornament. And He created what you do not know." (Holy Quran 16:5-8)

1. Field of Study: _____

    a) Area of Study:

_____

_____

_____

_____

    b) Problem No. ____:

    c) Derived Industries:

_____

_____

_____

_____

    d) Economic (or social benefit) potential:

_____

_____

_____

_____

    e) Educational requirements:

_____

_____

2. Field of Study: _____

    a) Area of Study:

_____

_____

_____

_____

    b) Problem No. ____:

    c) Derived Industries:

_____

_____

_____

_____

    d) Economic (or social benefit) potential:

_____

_____

_____

_____

    e) Educational requirements:

_____

_____

_____

_____

5. The uncle of Mr. W.D. Fard lives in the wilderness of North America and he is living other than himself, therefore, he weighs more than his height and his blood pressure registers more than thirty-two. This killed him at the age of forty-four years....

| threpsology | science of nutrition |
| trophology | study of nutrition |

"And from the fruits of date palm and grapes you get wholesome drink and nutrition: Behold in this is a sign for those who are wise" (Holy Quran 16:67)

1. Field of Study: _____

   a) Area of Study:

_____

_____

_____

   b) Problem No. ____:

   c) Derived Industries:

_____

_____

_____

   d) Economic (or social benefit) potential:

_____

_____

e) Educational requirements:

_____

_____

_____

_____

2. Field of Study: _____

a) Area of Study:

_____

_____

_____

_____

b) Problem No. ____:

c) Derived Industries:

_____

_____

_____

_____

d) Economic (or social benefit) potential:

_____

_____

_____

_____

82

e) Educational requirements:

_____

_____

_____

_____

6. The second uncle of Mr. W.D. Fard, in the wilderness of North America, lived other than himself and, therefore, his blood pressure registered over thirty-two. He had fever, headaches, chills, grippe, hay fever, regular fever, rheumatism; also pain in all joints. He was disturbed with foot ailments and toothaches....

If the air value selling price, then the third uncle of Mr. W.D. Fard would have been robbed of the Atmosphere. How much air did he breathe more than the average man? Each cubic foot of air costs $10.50.

How much does Mr. W.D. Fard's second uncle robbed in forty-six years? Twenty pills cost twenty-five cents. How much does this amount to in forty-six years?.....

odontology	study of teeth
virology	study of viruses
periodontics	study of gums
pyretology	study of fevers
rheumatology	study of rheumatism
palynology	study of pollen
osteology	study of bones
parasitology	study of parasites
podology	study of the feet
koniology	study of atmospheric pollutants and dust
pharmacology	study of drugs
posology	science of quantity or dosage
acology	study of medical remedies
anaesthesiology	study of anaesthetics

"Everything good that happens to you (O Man) is from God, everything bad that happens to you is from your own actions". (Holy Quran 4:79).

1. Field of Study: _____

a) Area of Study:

_____

_____

_____

_____

b) Problem No. ____:

c) Derived Industries:

_____

_____

_____

_____

d) Economic (or social benefit) potential:

_____

_____

_____

_____

e) Educational requirements:

_____

_____

_____

_____

2. Field of Study: _____

a) Area of Study:

_____

_____

_____

_____

b) Problem No. ____:

c) Derived Industries:

_____

_____

_____

_____

d) Economic (or social benefit) potential:

_____

_____

_____

_____

e) Educational requirements:

_____

_____

_____

_____

3. Field of Study: _____

a) Area of Study:

_____

_____

_____

_____

b) Problem No. _____:

c) Derived Industries:

_____

_____

_____

_____

d) Economic (or social benefit) potential:

_____

_____

_____

_____

e) Educational requirements:

_____

_____

_____

_____

4. Field of Study: _____

a) Area of Study:

_____

_____

_____

_____

b) Problem No. _____ :

c) Derived Industries:

_____

_____

_____

_____

d) Economic (or social benefit) potential:

_____

_____

_____

_____

e) Educational requirements:

_____

_____

_____

_____

7. If one one-hundred of a cubic of a inch contains two hundred million atoms, the total Atmosphere weighs eleven and two-thirds quintillion pounds. One-third of eleven and two thirds quintillion pounds equal atoms. Mr. Muhammad cracked one atom into ten million parts. Then Mr. Sharrieff wants to know what will be the weight of the cracked Atom?

$100.00 (In Gold) For The Person Who Works This Problem (Qualified Muslims)

aerology	study of the atmosphere
physics	study of properties of matter and energy
barology	study of gravitation
mechanics	study of action of force on bodies
metallogeny	study of the origin and distribution of metal deposits
metallography	study of the structure and constitution of metals
metallurgy	study of alloying and treating metals
chrysology	study of precious metals

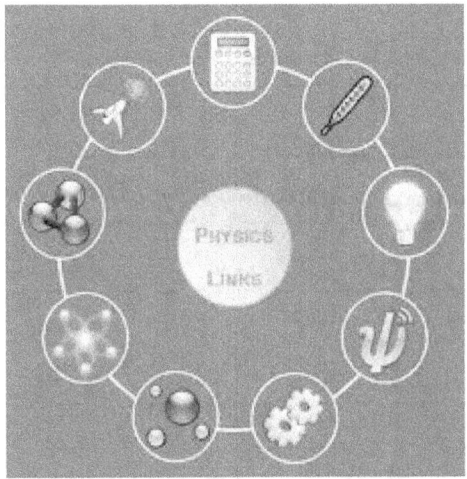

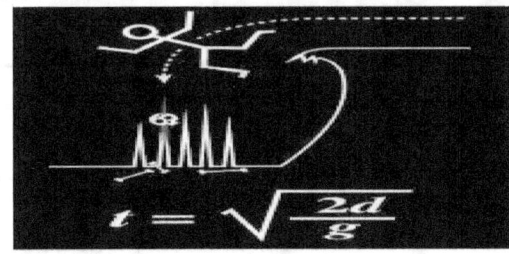

$$t = \sqrt{\frac{2d}{g}}$$

"Say, "Travel in the earth and find out how He originated creation. And how afterward, Allah brings forth entirely new forms. Verily, Allah is the Designer of all things." (Holy Quran 29:20)

1. Field of Study: _____

   a) Area of Study:

_____

_____

b) Problem No.____ :

c) Derived Industries:

_____

_____

_____

_____

d) Economic (or social benefit) potential:

_____

_____

_____

_____

e) Educational requirements:

_____

_____

_____

_____

2. *Field of Study*: _____

a) Area of Study:

_____

_____

b) Problem No.____:

c) Derived Industries:

d) Economic (or social benefit) potential:

e) Educational requirements:

3. *Field of Study*: _____

a) Area of Study:

_____

_____

b) Problem No.____:

c) Derived Industries:

_____

_____

_____

_____

d) Economic (or social benefit) potential:

_____

_____

_____

_____

e) Educational requirements:

_____

_____

_____

_____

4. *Field of Study*: _____

a) Area of Study:

_____

_____

b) Problem No. ____:

c) Derived Industries:

d) Economic (or social benefit) potential:

e) Educational requirements:

9. The population of Detroit is one million five hundred thousand people, and there are two hundred and fifty thousand original nation.

During these hard times for the lack of jobs, not having enough money to buy food, they eat two meals per day...

It is also known to the civilized world that ten ounces of the poison animal destroys three one-hundredths percent of the beauty appearance of a person. Then Mr. Muhammad wants to know how long will it take to destroy the whole one hundred percent of the beauty appearance at the above eating rates?

proaxeology	study of practical or efficient activity; science of efficient action
euthenics	science concerned with improving living conditions
urbanology	study of cities
ethonomics	study of economic and ethical principles of a society
dermatology	study of skin
kalology	study of beauty

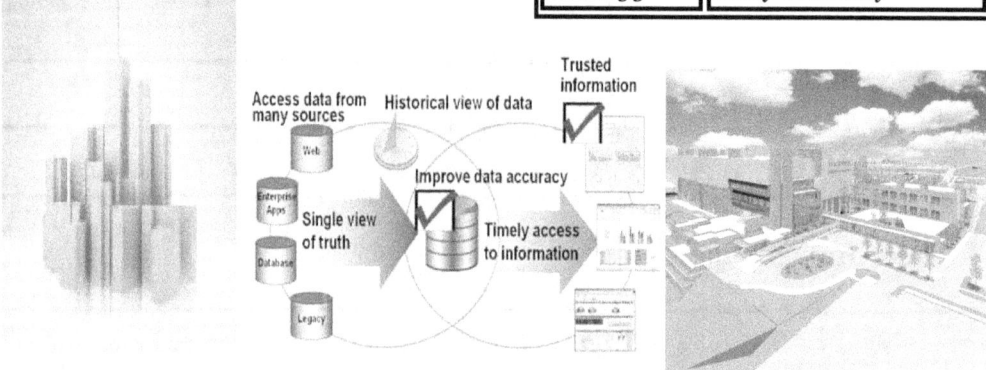

"Truly, God does not change the condition of a people until they change what is in themselves." (Holy Quran 13:11)

1. Field of Study: _____

   a) Area of Study:

_____

_____

_____

_____

b) Problem No.____:

c) Derived Industries:

_____

_____

_____

_____

d) Economic (or social benefit) potential:

_____

_____

_____

e) Educational requirements:

_____

_____

_____

_____

2. Field of Study: _____

a) Area of Study:

_____

_____

_____

_____

b) Problem No.____:

c) Derived Industries:

_____

_____

_____

_____

d) Economic (or social benefit) potential:

_____

_____

_____

_____

e) Educational requirements:

_____

_____

_____

_____

3. *Field of Study*: _____

a) Area of Study:

_____

_____

_____

_____

b) Problem No.____:

c) Derived Industries:

_____

_____

_____

_____

d) Economic (or social benefit) potential:

_____

_____

_____

_____

e) Educational requirements:

_____

_____

_____

_____

Lessons of W.D. Fard	Corresponding Sciences/Fields of Study

11. The Suez Canal in Egypt is ninety miles long, with a depth of thirty-three feet, and a width of one hundred twenty-two feet. The cost to build it sixty-four years ago was one hundred fifty million dollars. Mr. A. Ali has five hundred dollars worth of stock in it at the rate of six and three-fifths percent. Now he wants to know how much money he has coming to him at the above rate from 1869 to May 26, 1933...

notaphily	collecting of bank-notes and cheques
catalactics	science of commercial exchange

"Who gives his wealth (for the benefits of others) so that he may attain self-development and grow in goodness." (Holy Quran 92:18)

1. *Field of Study*: catalactics

    a) Area of Study: science of commercial exchange

    b) Problem #11: Mr. A. Ali has five hundred dollars worth of stock in it at the rate of six and three-fifths percent....how much money he has coming to him at the above rate...

    c) Derived Industries: International Banks, Commercial Banks, Public Banks, Stock exchange, jobs......

    d) Economic (or social benefit) potential: Friedrich Hayek used the term Catallaxy to describe a market economy. He was unhappy with the usage of the word "economy", feeling that the Greek root of the word - which translates as "household management" - implied that economic agents in a market economy possessed shared goals. Hayek derived the word Catallaxy from the Greek verb "katallassein" (or "katallattein") which meant not only "to exchange" but also "to admit in the community" and "to change from enemy into friend" (F.A. von Hayek, Law legislation and Liberty, Vol 2, 1976, pp. 108-109).

    e) Education requirements: Mathematics, Scarcity, Choice, Opportunity Cost, Specialization, Spending, Producers/Production, Consumers/Consumption, Factors of Production, Markets, Prices, Trade-offs, Demand, Supply, Competition, Equilibrium Price, Entrepreneurs, Money, Currencies, Finance, Personal Finance, Macro Data, Employment, Government Budgets, and Debt, Stocks, Funds Company Data, Population and Places, General Social Sciences/Educational, Government and Political, Econometics, International Data...

"The example of those who spend their monies in the cause of GOD is that of a grain that produces seven spikes, with a hundred grains in each spike. GOD multiplies this manifold for whomever He wills. GOD is Bounteous, Knower." (Holy Quran 2:261)

2. *Field of Study*: _____

a) Area of Study:

_____

_____

_____

_____

b) Problem No.____:

c) Derived Industries:

_____

_____

_____

_____

d) Economic (or social benefit) potential:

_____

_____

_____

_____

e) Educational requirements:

_____

_____

_____

_____

12. The Area of the Planet is one hundred ninety-six million, nine hundred forty thousand square miles and she weighs six sextillion tons. Mr. Shah wants to know how much does the State of Michigan weigh? Going by the Book Of Darkness – saying that the State of Michigan is fifty-seven thousand, nine hundred eighty square miles and has a population of four million, eight hundred forty-two thousand, two hundred eighty people...

One cubic foot of common Earth weighs eighty pounds. One common Ca. weighs one hundred seventy pounds. The average original weighs one hundred fifty pounds and there are five hundred thousand original nations living in the State of Michigan; approximately eight million live stock of all kinds....

Don't tell her that there was no one to teach you for three hundred and seventy -nine years. She already knows and is trying to forget it. Now she will teach you quickly any course you may desire.

geography	study of surface of the earth and its inhabitants
zoopathology	study of animal diseases
zoogeography	study of geographic distribution of animals
zootechnics	science of breeding animals
rhochrematics	science of inventory management and the movement of products

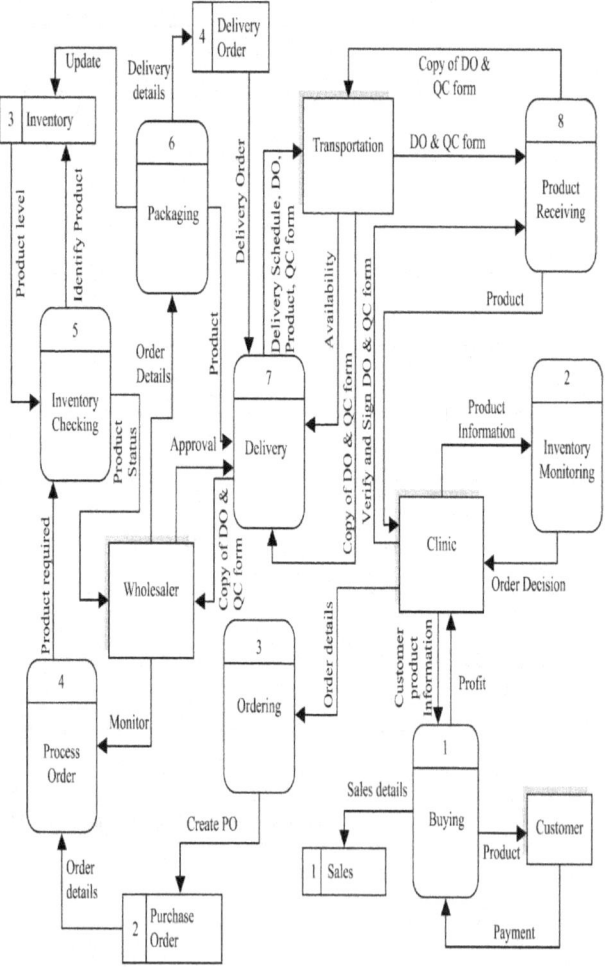

"GOD bears witness that there is no god except He, and so do the angels and those who possess knowledge. Truthfully and equitably, He is the absolute god; there is no god but He, the Almighty, Most Wise." (Holy Quran 3:18)

1. Field of Study: _____

a) Area of Study:

_____

_____

_____

_____

b) Problem No.____:

c) Derived Industries:

_____

_____

_____

_____

d) Economic (or social benefit) potential:

_____

_____

_____

_____

e) Educational requirements:

_____

_____

_____

_____

2. *Field of Study*: _____

a) Area of Study:

_____

_____

_____

_____

b) Problem No.____:

c) Derived Industries:

_____

_____

_____

_____

d) Economic (or social benefit) potential:

_____

_____

_____

e) Educational requirements:

_____

_____

_____

_____

13. After learning Mathematics, which is Islam, and Islam is Mathematics, it stands true. You can always prove it at no limit of time. Then you must learn to use it and secure some benefit while you are living – that is luxury, money, good homes, friendships in all walks of life....

Now you must speak the Language so you can use your mathematical Theology in the proper term, otherwise you will not be successful...

There are twenty-six letters in the Language and if a Student Learns one letter per day, then how long will it take him to learn the twenty-six letters?

There are ten numbers in the Mathematic Language. Then how long will it take a Student to learn the whole ten numbers (at the above rate?)

mathematics	study of magnitude, number, and forms
economics	study of material wealth
chrematistics	the study of wealth; political economy
tonetics	study of pronunciation
phonology	study of speech sounds
phoniatrics	study and correction of speech defects
numerology	study of numbers

"Only to a messenger that He chooses, does He reveal from the past and the future, specific news. This is to ascertain that they have delivered their Lord's messages. He is fully aware of what they have. He has counted the numbers of all things." (Holy Quran 72:27-28)

1. Field of Study: _____

    a) Area of Study:

_____

_____

_____

_____

b) Problem No.____:

c) Derived Industries:

_____

_____

_____

_____

d) Economic (or social benefit) potential:

_____

_____

_____

_____

e) Educational requirements:

_____

_____

_____

_____

2. *Field of Study*: _____

a) Area of Study:

_____

_____

_____

_____

b) Problem No.____:

c) Derived Industries:

_____

_____

_____

_____

d) Economic (or social benefit) potential:

_____

_____

_____

_____

e) Educational requirements:

_____

_____

_____

_____

3. *Field of Study*: _____

a) Area of Study:

_____

_____

_____

_____

b) Problem No._____:

c) Derived Industries:

_____

_____

_____

_____

d) Economic (or social benefit) potential:

_____

_____

_____

_____

e) Educational requirements:

_____

_____

_____

_____

14. The University of Al-Azhar, in Cairo, has a Student population of thirty-six hundred; all but one-tenth taking other than language, three-tenths taking Construction Engineering, two-tenths taking Civil Engineering, three-tenths taking Mechanical Engineering, and the rest taking Teachership.

Egyptology	study of ancient Egypt
electrology	study of electricity
glossology	study of language; study of the tongue
ichnography	art of drawing ground plans
lexicology	study of words and their meanings
lexigraphy	art of definition of words
linguistics	study of language
ideogeny	study of origins of ideas
orthoepy	study of correct pronunciation
orthography	study of spelling
syntax	study of sentence structure

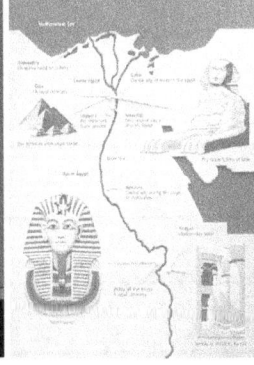

"Read, in the name of your Lord, who created." (Holy Quran 96:1)

1. Field of Study: _____

   a) Area of Study:

   _____

   _____

   _____

   _____

   b) Problem No._____:

   c) Derived Industries:

   _____

   _____

_____

_____

d) Economic (or social benefit) potential:

_____

_____

_____

_____

e) Educational requirements:

_____

_____

_____

_____

2. *Field of Study*: _____

a) Area of Study:

_____

_____

_____

_____

b) Problem No.____:

c) Derived Industries:

_____

_____

d) Economic (or social benefit) potential:

_____

_____

_____

_____

e) Educational requirements:

_____

_____

_____

_____

3. *Field of Study*: _____

a) Area of Study:

_____

_____

_____

_____

b) Problem No.____:

c) Derived Industries:

_____

_____

_____

_____

d) Economic (or social benefit) potential:

_____

_____

_____

_____

e) Educational requirements:

_____

_____

_____

_____

17. Mars, the inhabited Planet, is one hundred forty-one million, five hundred thousand miles from the Sun, and she travels one thousand thirty-seven and one-third miles per hour. Her diameter is four thousand two hundred miles. ...

18. Mercury is also an inhabited Planet and is thirty-six million miles from the Sun. Her diameter is three thousand miles.....

24. Platoon is four billion, six hundred million miles from the Sun and she travels the same rate around the Sun as the rest of the Planets. It takes her three hundred forty-five years to make on complete circle around the Sun...

areology	study of Mars
planetology	study of planets
astrogeology	study of extraterrestrial geology
uranology	study of the heavens; astronomy
astronomy	study of celestial bodies
astrophysics	study of behaviour of interstellar matter
astroseismology	study of star oscillations
uranography	descriptive astronomy and mapping
statics	study of bodies and forces in equilibrium

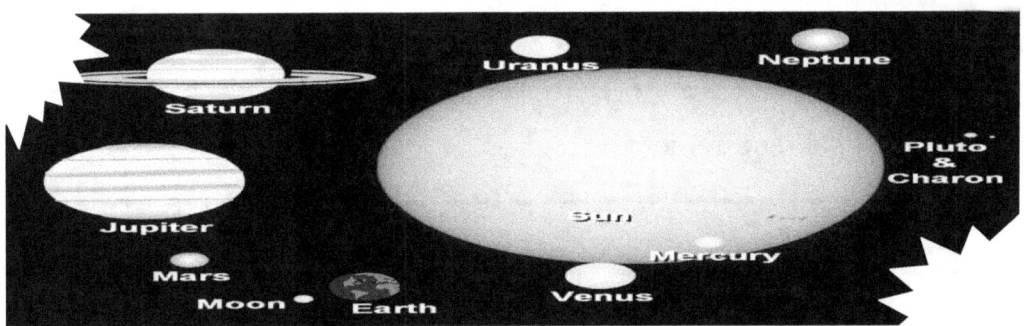

"Do you not see that GOD has committed in your service everything in the heavens and the earth, and has showered you with His blessings - obvious and hidden? Yet, some people argue about GOD without knowledge, without guidance, and without the enlightening scripture." (Holy Quran 31:20)

1. Field of Study: _____

    a) Area of Study:

_____

_____

_____

_____

b) Problem No.____:

c) Derived Industries:

_____

_____

_____

_____

d) Economic (or social benefit) potential:

_____

_____

_____

_____

e) Educational requirements:

_____

_____

_____

_____

2. Field of Study: _____

a) Area of Study:

_____

_____

_____

_____

b) Problem No.____:

c) Derived Industries:

_____

_____

_____

_____

d) Economic (or social benefit) potential:

_____

_____

_____

_____

e) Educational requirements:

_____

_____

_____

_____

112

30. The uncle of Mr. W.D. Fard lives in the wilderness of North America, surrounded and robbed completely by the Cave man. Therefore, he has no knowledge of his own nor anyone else's, but his mind travels twenty-four billion miles per second, which is considered the average speed of thought per second.

How many round trips will he make in ten seconds to the far Planet Platoon?

victimology	study of victims
nomology	the science of the laws; especially of the mind
metaphysics	study of principles of nature and thought
metapsychology	study of nature of the mind
neuropsychology	study of relation between brain and behaviour
psychobiology	study of biology of the mind
psychology	study of mind
psychophysics	study of link between mental and physical processes

"O you who believe stand out firmly for justice as witnesses to God (Allah) even as against yourselves or your parents or your kin." (Holy Quran 4:135)

1. Field of Study: _____

a) Area of Study:

_____

_____

_____

_____

b) Problem No.____:

c) Derived Industries:

_____

_____

_____

_____

d) Economic (or social benefit) potential:

_____

_____

_____

_____

e) Educational requirements:

_____

_____

_____

_____

2. Field of Study: _____

a) Area of Study:

_____

_____

_____

_____

b) Problem No.____:

c) Derived Industries:

_____

_____

_____

_____

d) Economic (or social benefit) potential:

_____

_____

_____

_____

e) Educational requirements:

_____

_____

_____

_____

3. Field of Study: _____

a) Area of Study:

_____

_____

_____

_____

b) Problem No.____:

c) Derived Industries:

_____

_____

_____

_____

d) Economic (or social benefit) potential:

_____

_____

_____

_____

e) Educational requirements:

_____

_____

_____

_____

31. A lion in a cage walks back and forth, sixty feet per minute, seeking a way out of the cage. It took nearly four centuries to find the door. Now, with modern equipment, he is walking three thousand feet per minute and he has three thousand miles by two thousand miles to go yet. How long will it take him to cover this territory of said, three thousand by two thousand miles, at the above walking rate? Five thousand two hundred eight feet equals one mile....

psychoacousitics	recovery of messages by brain
homiletics	the art of preaching
metapolitics	study of politics in theory or abstract
stasiology	study of political parties
ergology	study of effects of work on humans
noology	science of the intellect

32. Twelve Leaders of Islam from all over the Planet have conferred in the Root of Civilization concerning the Lost Found Nation of Islam; must return to their original Land.

One of the Conference Members, by the name of Mr. Osman Sharrieff, said to the eleven Members of the Conference: "The Lost Found Nation of Islam will not return to their original land unless they, first, have a thorough knowledge of their own". So they sent a Messenger to them of their own.

Now, the Messenger and his Labors worked day and night for the last three and one-half years, and their accomplishment is approximately twenty-five thousand. The Messenger and his Labors are worried, for the time of Laboring is mentioned and limited in said, Problem No. 31.

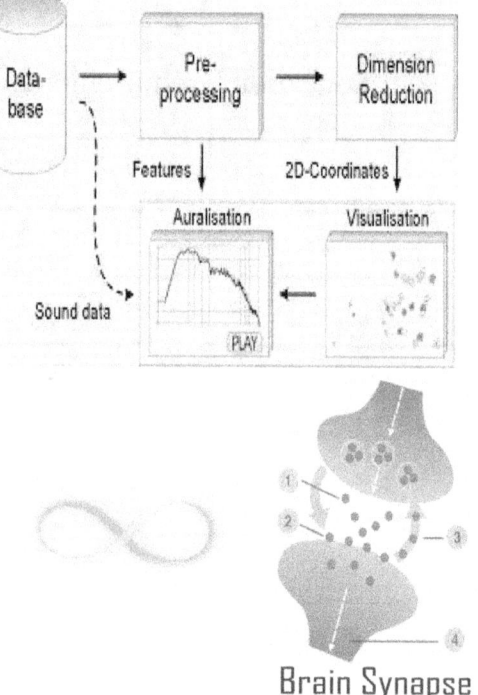

One of the Prophets in the early days said: "The Lost Found Nation of Islam numbering one hundred forty-four thousand, will be Stars, and will return to their original Land. And the Balance", he said, "are poison and rusty, and will not take the Knowledge of their own".

Brain Synapse

But the Messenger and his Labors do not agree with the old Prophets in this modern time. ...

"And do not follow (blindly) any information of which you have no (direct) knowledge. (Using your faculties of perception and conception, you must verify it for yourself. (In the Court of your Lord,) you will be held accountable for your hearing, sight, and the faculty of reasoning."(Holy Quran 17:36)

1. *Field of Study*: _____

a) Area of Study:

_____

_____

_____

_____

b) Problem No.____:

c) Derived Industries:

_____

_____

_____

_____

d) Economic (or social benefit) potential:

_____

_____

_____

_____

e) Educational requirements:

_____

_____

_____

_____

33. Lake Michigan is three hundred nine and one-third miles long, sixty-nine and one half miles wide, and she has a depth of eight hundred sixty-eight and one fourth feet. What would be the square mileage of this Cave man's Lake? Reduce to square Yards and inches.

One thousand seven hundred twenty-eight cubic inches equal one cubic foot. One gallon of water contains two hundred thirty-one cubic inches. On cubic foot of water contains seven and one half gallons. One thousand seven hundred twenty-eight cubic inches of water weigh sixty-two and one-half pounds.

Mr. E. Muhammad wants to know if thirteen Ducks – six drink one ounce per day and seven drink three-fourth ounces per day, how long will it take them to dry the Cave Man's Lake? What would be the total weight of water in this Cave man's Lake? Extract the cube root of the total amount of water after having all dry by the thirteen Ducks.

hydrography	study of investigating bodies of water
hydrogeology	study of ground water
hydrology	study of water resources
metrology	science of weights and measures
neossology	study of nestling birds
ornithology	study of birds

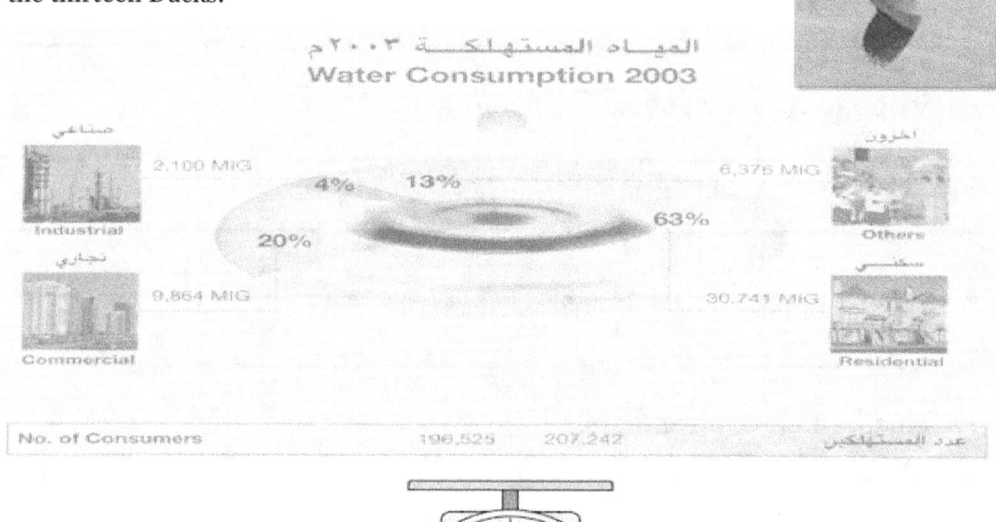

"There is no animal on the earth, no bird which flies on wings, that (does not belong to) communities like you. We have not neglected anything in the Book (of Decrees). Then to their Lord they will be gathered." (Holy Quran 6:38)

1. Field of Study: _____

    a) Area of Study:

_____

_____

_____

_____

    b) Problem No._____:

    c) Derived Industries:

_____

_____

_____

_____

    d) Economic (or social benefit) potential:

_____

_____

_____

_____

    e) Educational requirements:

_____

_____

_____

_____

34. The uncle of Mr. W.D. Fard lives in the wilderness of North America and works sixteen hours out of twenty-four every day for a very little day. He has a large family to support and, on top of that, a Satan came along and sold him Life insurance, and gave him a written Guarantee that he will receive a full benefit at once on after approval of his death.

Another Satan came along and sold him five hundred B. Shares at six percent, in the Panama Canal, at $1.75 per Share. The Panama Canal was completed in 1914 at a cost of $375,000,000. Mostly the bigger part of the sum belongs to the Share-Holders, whom we call the 85%.

The Panama Canal is fifty and one-half miles long, three hundred feet wide and has a depth of forty-five feet. What would be the amount of water in weight and gallons belonging to the uncle of Mr. W.D. Fard since there were nine thousand, nine hundred fifty-seven Share-Holders, not including the 15%.

ethonomics	study of economic and ethical principles of a society
catalactics	science of commercial exchange
cambistry	science of international exchange
scripophily	collection of bond and share certificates

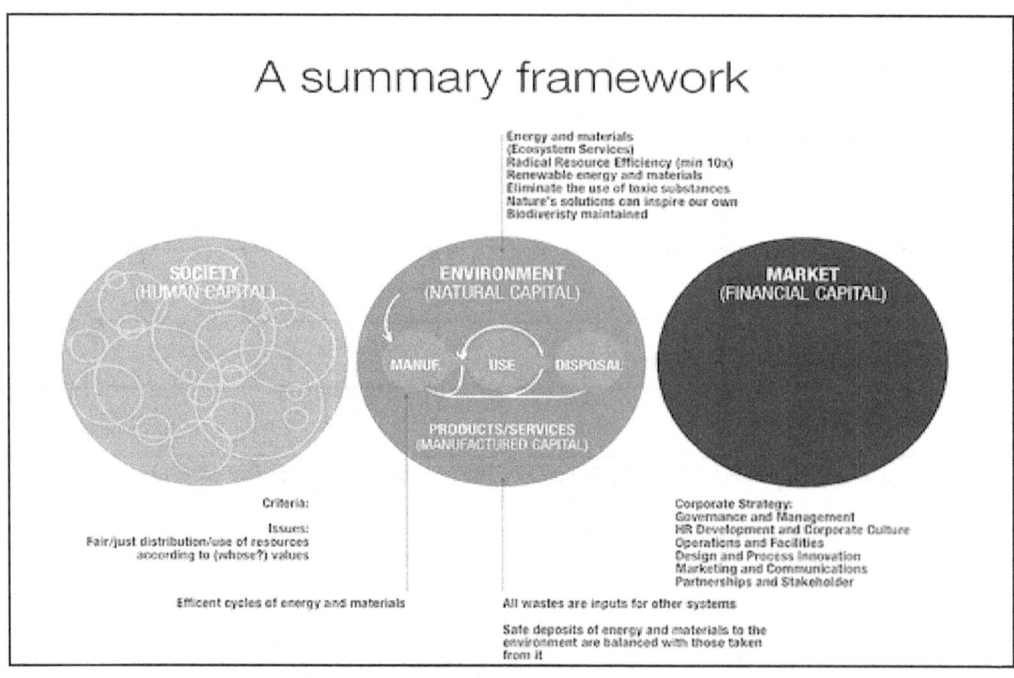

"O ye who believe! Eat not up your property among yourselves in vanities; but let there be among you traffic and trade by mutual good-will". (Holy Quran 4:29)

1. Field of Study: _____

a) Area of Study:

_____

_____

_____

_____

b) Problem No.____:

c) Derived Industries:

_____

_____

_____

_____

d) Economic (or social benefit) potential:

_____

_____

_____

_____

e) Educational requirements:

_____

_____

_____

_____

2. Field of Study: _____

   a) Area of Study:

_____

_____

_____

_____

   b) Problem No.____:

   c) Derived Industries:

_____

_____

_____

_____

   d) Economic (or social benefit) potential:

_____

_____

_____

_____

   e) Educational requirements:

_____

_____

Assignment 6

English Lesson C-1

Read what is called English Lesson No. C1. The concept of "intelligence gathering" will come to mind. This particular lesson represents the intelligence gathering that Master Wallace D. Fard Muhammad conveyed regarding the lost tribe and those whom had brought them to North America as slaves thereby ordering the need for Supreme Wisdom to guide a new developing nation[s].

Lessons written by W.D. Fard (a.k.a. W.F. Muhammad)

1. My name is W. F. Muhammad. (a.k.a. W. D. Fard)
2. I came to North America by myself.
3. My uncle was brought over here by the Trader three hundred seventy-nine years ago.
4. My uncle cannot talk his own language.
5. He does not know that he is my uncle.
6. He likes the devil because the devil gives him nothing.
7. Why does he like the devil?
8. Because the devil put fear in him when he was a little boy.
9. Why does he fear, now since he is a big man?
10. Because the devil taught him to eat the wrong food.
11. Does that have anything to do with the above question, No. 10?
12. Yes sir. That makes him other than his own self.
13. What is his own self?
14. His own self is a righteous Muslim.
15. Are there any Muslims other than righteous?
16. I beg your pardon. I have never heard of one.
17. How many Muslim sons are there in North America?
18. Approximately three million.
19. How many original Muslims are there in North America?
20. A little over seventeen million.
21. Did I hear you say that some of the seventeen million do not know that they are Muslims?
22. YES SIR.
23. I hardly believe that unless they are blind, deaf and dumb.
24. Well, they were made blind, deaf and dumb by the devil when they were babies.
25. CAN THE DEVIL FOOL A MUSLIM?

26. NOT NOWADAYS.
27. Do you mean to say the devil fooled them three hundred
    seventy-nine years ago?
28. Yes, the TRADER made an interpretation that they receive
    GOLD for their labor, more then they were earning in their own
    country.
29. Then did they receive gold?
30. NO. The Trader disappeared and there was no one that could
    speak their language.
31. Then what happened?
32. WELL, they wanted to go to their own country, but they could
    not swim nine thousand miles.
33. Why didn't their own people come and get them?
34. Because their own people did not know that they were here.
35. When did there own people find out that they were here?
36. Approximately sixty years ago.

So what is "intelligence gathering?" Simply put, it's a
cycle, which is made up of discrete steps, and expected to yield
a specific product. Along the way, however, there may be
obstacles or barriers to reaching the next step and/or the
finished product. Problems may exist in obtaining reliable
"inputs" for the systematic flow of information needed to
produce an "output," and such reliability problems are usually
discovered in the ANALYSIS phase -- more completely
described as the process of evaluating data for reliability,
validity, and relevance; integrating and analyzing it; and
converting the product of this effort into a meaningful whole...
(Johnson 2005) As another alternative to the traditional model
of the intelligence cycle, Lowenthal (2006) has proposed
adding the CONSUMPTION and FEEDBACK phase. Often, a
layered approach is used by the intelligence community to
convey the same intelligence in different formats to
policymakers. This final phase would ensure that the right
amount of detail is included in the various formats, and that
consumers are receiving the kind of intelligence they need. In
short, there are five groups with a relatively permanent
"agenda" for any intelligence agency:

"O you who believe, you shall avoid any suspicion, for even a little bit of suspicion is sinful. You shall not spy on one another, nor shall you backbite one another; this is as abominable as eating the flesh of your dead brother. You certainly abhor this. You shall observe GOD. GOD is Redeemer, Most Merciful."
(Holy Quran 49:12)

Field of Study: <u>INTELLIGENCE</u>

1. Field of Study: _____

    a) Area of Study:

_____

_____

_____

_____

    b) English Lesson C-1 No.<u>1-36</u>

    c) Derived Industries:

_____

_____

_____

_____

    d) Economic (or social benefit) potential:

_____

_____

_____

_____

e) Educational requirements:

_____

_____

_____

_____

Recommended Reading

www.ingramcontent.com/pod-product-compliance
Lightning Source LLC
Chambersburg PA
CBHW081354280526
45788CB00009B/2876